Crafts from
Your Favorite

BY KATHY ROSS

illustrated by Vicky Enright

The Millbrook Press   Brookfield, Connecticut

To Elm, whose musical talent is just one of
many of his gifts that I have enjoyed
—KR

To my two favorite singers,
Sean and his dad
—VE

Library of Congress Cataloging-in-Publication Data
Ross, Kathy (Katharine Reynolds), 1948–
Crafts from your favorite children's songs / by Kathy Ross;
illustrated by Vicky Enright.
p. cm.
Includes bibliographical references.
Summary: Provides directions for creating puppets, games, jewelry, toys, and
other projects related to such favorite children's songs as "Old MacDonald
Had a Farm," "The Eensy, Weensy Spider," and "Rock-a-bye-Baby."
ISBN 0-7613-1912-3 (lib. bdg.) 0-7613-1438-5 (pbk.)
1. Handicraft—Juvenile literature. 2. Children's songs—Juvenile literature.
[1. Handicraft.] I. Enright, Vicky, ill. II. Title.
TT160.R7142276 2001
745.5—dc21 00-021228

Published by The Millbrook Press, Inc.
2 Old New Milford Road
Brookfield, Connecticut 06804
www.millbrookpress.com

Contents

Introduction

The selection of traditional songs for American children is a work in progress. Nursery rhymes sung in the early part of the twentieth century have not been replaced but, rather, joined by newer songs that tell about spiders, buses, and feelings.

Children love to participate and so it is no coincidence that several of the songs I've chosen to include in this book are interactive. My own nursery school students love to make faces during "If You're Happy and You Know It..." or to dramatically whoosh the Itsy, Bitsy Spider down the water spout. And, of course, the "all fall down" segment of "Ring Around the Rosie" is a direct invitation for a case of classroom giggles. With this book, I have extended the fun of some of my favorite tunes with craft projects that reflect the charm, humor, and sometimes the outright silliness of the songs. The children will not only have the fun of creating the crafts but also of using them to enhance the singing of the songs.

Since the selected songs are mainly familiar ones, I have not provided the words and music, although they are available in a number of standard collections and on the Web. Also, some of the individual songs are the subject of delightful picturebooks. Here is a list of my favorites:

Adams, Pam, illus. *Old MacDonald Had a Farm.* Auburn, ME: Child's Play International, 1990.

Amery, Heather. *The Usborne Children's Song Book.* Tulsa, OK: EDC Publishing, 1989.

Appleby, Amy. *The Library of Children's Song Classics.* New York: Omnibus Press, 1993.

Carter, David A., *If You're Happy and You Know It, Clap Your Hands: A Pop-Up Book.* New York: Scholastic, 1997.

Eagle, Kin. *It's Raining, It's Pouring.* Watertown, MA: Charlesbridge, 1997.

Fox, Dan. *Go In and Out the Window.* New York: Henry Holt, 1987.

The Giant Book of Children's Songs. New York: Cherry Lane Music Company, 1995.

Litzinger, Rosanne, illus. *The Wheels on the Bus.* Brookfield, CT: Millbrook Press, 1999.

Manning, Jane K. *My First Songs.* New York: HarperCollins, 1998.

The Really Big Book of Children's Songs. Milwaukee: Hal Leonard Corp., 1998.

Trapani, Iza, and Jane Taylor, illus. *Twinkle, Twinkle Little Star.* Watertown, MA: Charlesbridge Publishing, 1998.

Trapani, Iza, illus. *The Itsy, Bitsy Spider.* Watertown, MA: Charlesbridge Publishing, 1997.

————————— *I'm a Little Teapot.* Watertown, MA: Charlesbridge Publishing, 1999.

Winn, Marie. *The Fireside Book of Children's Songs.* New York: Simon & Schuster, 1969.

Zelinsky, Paul O. *The Wheels on the Bus: The Traditional Song* (Pop-Up Edition). New York: Dutton Children's Books, 1990.

Have fun and keep on singing!

Kathy Ross

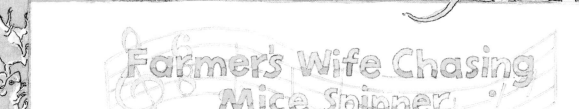

Farmer's Wife Chasing Mice Spinner

Here is what you need:

newspaper to work on

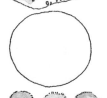

9-inch (23-cm) paper plate

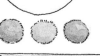

3 mouse-colored pom-poms

plastic straw

masking tape

markers and a sharp black permanent marker

cardboard toilet-tissue tube

blue poster paint and a paintbrush

scissors

ruler

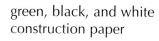

green, black, and white construction paper

white glue

black yarn

hole punch

Here is what you do:

1 Paint the bottom of the paper plate blue and let it dry.

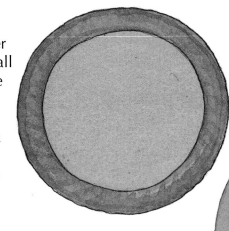

2 Cut a circle from the green construction paper about 1 inch (2.5 cm) smaller than the plate all the way around. Cut a 2-inch (5-cm) slit down the center of one end of the straw. Spread the two ends of the straw apart and tape them to the center of the green circle. The straw will be used as a handle for spinning the circle around. If you need to, you can strengthen the straw by wrapping it in masking tape.

3 Turn the three pom-poms into mice. Use the black marker to give each one eyes and a nose. Punch ears from the black paper and glue them on each mouse. Glue the three mice on one side of the edge of the green paper. Cut a 1-inch (2.5-cm) piece of yarn for each mouse and slip one under the back of each pom-pom mouse for a tail.

4 On the white paper, use the markers to draw and color a farmer's wife with her knife. Cut around the figure leaving a 2-inch (5-cm) strip of paper across the bottom to fold back and use to glue her to the green circle. You might want to color the other side of the figure, too. Fold back the tab at the bottom and glue the farmer's wife to the green circle on the opposite side from the mice.

5 Cut five 2-inch (5-cm)-long slits around one end of the cardboard tube. Spread the cut portion of the tube out and glue it to the center of the unpainted side of the plate. Use the masking tape to hold the tube in place while the glue dries.

6 Poke a hole in the center of the plate. Drop the end of the straw attached to the green circle through the tube so that the circle rests on the blue plate.

To make the farmer's wife run after the mice hold on to the tube with one hand and spin the straw around with the other.

"Did you ever see such a sight in your life?"

9

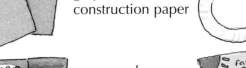

Bear Over The Mountain Puppet

Here is what you need:

 scissors

 ruler

white glue

gray and brown construction paper

 markers

2 paper fasteners

 9-inch (23-cm) paper plate

 cereal box cardboard

 dried coffee grounds

Here is what you do:

1 From the gray paper, cut a mountain shape large enough to cover the front of the paper plate.

the other side of the mountain

2 From the brown paper, cut a bear shape about 5 inches (13 cm) long. Use the markers to give the bear a face. Cover the bear with glue and sprinkle on dried coffee grounds for fur.

3 Cut a strip from the cereal box cardboard that is about 8 inches (20 cm) long and 1 1/2 inches (4 cm) wide. Using a paper fastener, attach the bear through its center to one end of the strip.

4 Set the mountain shape on top of the paper plate. Push another paper fastener through the center of the mountain and the plate. Then push the fastener through the end of the cardboard strip.

The bear can now go up and over the mountain

"to see what he can see."

Old MacDonald's Barn

Here is what you need:

 newspaper to work on

 red and brown poster paint and a paintbrush

 toilet-tissue tube

 scissors

 white glue

 large greeting card envelope

 cardboard egg carton

 construction paper in several colors

 markers

Here is what you do:

1 Paint the toilet-tissue tube red for the silo of the barn. If the envelope is not already red, paint that red, too.

2 Cut one cup from the cardboard egg carton. Paint the outside of it brown. Glue the cup to the top of the silo.

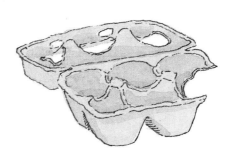

3 Open the flap of the envelope to form the roof of the barn. Glue the silo on one side of the front of the envelope.

4 Cut a double door and window for the barn from construction paper. Add details with the markers. Glue the door and window to the front of the envelope.

5 Draw all the animals on old MacDonald's farm on construction paper. Add details with the markers. Cut them out and slip them into the envelope barn.

As you sing the song "Old MacDonald Had a Farm" you can take each animal in the song out of the "barn" in turn.

Ee-i-Ee-i-oh!

A Pocket Full of Posies

Here is what you need:

 scissors

 white glue

kitchen-size paper cup

old shirt with a pocket

trim, ribbon, and lace

some real or artificial flowers

Here is what you do:

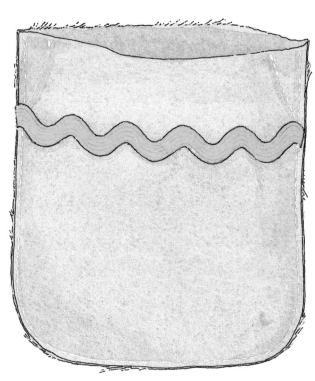

1 Cut the pocket off an old shirt. Decorate the pocket any way you wish, by gluing on trim, ribbon, and lace.

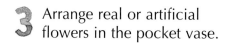

2 Slip the paper cup into the pocket. The cup will make the pocket stand upright and also provide a container for the flowers.

3 Arrange real or artificial flowers in the pocket vase.

Put some stones in the bottom of the cup so the posies don't

"all fall down."

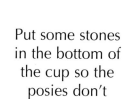

A pocket full of posies

15

The Old Man is Snoring Puppet

Here is what you need:

 newspaper to work on

 7-inch (18-cm) paper bowl

 poster paint in skin tone and a paintbrush

 scissors

 white glue

 balloon

 black and red markers

 construction paper in skin tone

 cotton balls

Here is what you do:

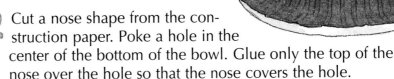

1 Paint the bottom of the bowl in the skin tone of your choice for the face of the old man.

2 Cut a nose shape from the construction paper. Poke a hole in the center of the bottom of the bowl. Glue only the top of the nose over the hole so that the nose covers the hole.

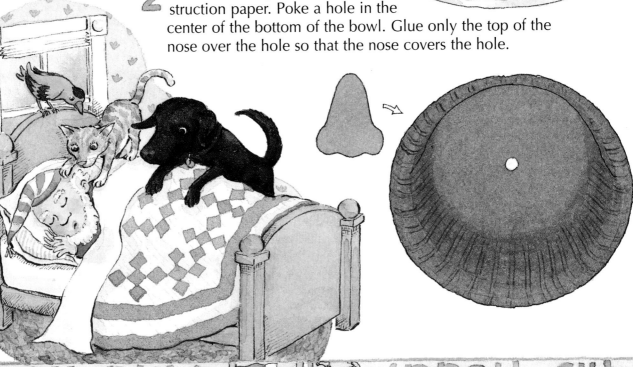

3 Use the markers to draw closed eyes and a mouth on the face.

4 Glue cotton balls around the bottom rim of the face for a beard for the old man.

5 Push the open end of the balloon through the hole from the back of the face so that it is underneath the nose.

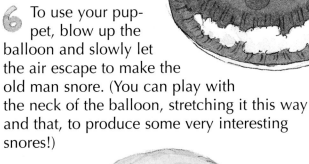

6 To use your puppet, blow up the balloon and slowly let the air escape to make the old man snore. (You can play with the neck of the balloon, stretching it this way and that, to produce some very interesting snores!)

zzZZZ

17

Twinkle Star Finger Puppet

Here is what you need:

 red permanent marker

 white glue

 unwanted shiny CD disk

 2 large wiggle eyes

 scissors

 masking tape

Here is what you do:

1 Draw the shape of the star on the back of the disk with the marker, and then cut the star out. It must be cut with adult scissors, so you may need to ask a grown-up for help with this part.

2 Use the red marker to draw a smile on the shiny side of the star just below the hole.

3 Put a small strip of masking tape above the hole. Put a small piece of tape on the back of each wiggle eye. This will help create a better gluing surface between the disk and the wiggle eyes. Glue the eyes on to the star on top of the masking tape.

Put your finger through the hole from the back of the disk, so that your finger forms a nose for the star. Hold your star

"up above the world so high"

and watch the shiny surface twinkle.

Black Sheep Lapel Pin

Here is what you need:

black 12-inch (30-cm) pipe cleaner

black yarn

scissors

2 seed beads

white glue

thin ribbon

gold safety pin

Here is what you do:

1 Fold the black pipe cleaner into the frame of a sheep. Starting at one end, bend first one leg then the other. Fold the end down to make the back, then fold two legs for the front of the sheep. Bring the end up and fold it over to make the head. Trim off any extra pipe cleaner.

2 Tie one end of a long piece of yarn to the body of the sheep. Start wrapping the yarn around and around the body to fill the sheep out. If you run out of yarn before you think the sheep is plump enough just tie on another piece. Wrap the neck and top of the head a couple of times, leaving the end of the pipe cleaner head sticking out for the face of the sheep. Tie off the end of the yarn when you are done wrapping.

3 Tie a ribbon around the neck of the sheep.

4 Glue two seed bead eyes to the face of the sheep.

5 Slip the back of the safety pin under some of the yarn strands along the side of the sheep, so you can wear him on your collar.

This is a very tiny black sheep. He probably won't have

"three bags full"

of wool.

21

Jack-in-the-Box Pop-Up

Here is what you need:

scissors

white glue

sliding matchbox

rubber band

blue construction paper

trims

markers

red yarn

Here is what you do:

1 Cut a strip of construction paper just big enough to cover the outside of the matchbox. Glue the paper around the matchbox.

Use the rubber band to hold the paper in place while the glue dries.

2 Decorate the outside of the box with bands of trim.

3 Use the markers to draw a face on the bottom of the inside box.

4 Cut bits of red yarn. Glue the bits to the top edge of the inner box above the face.

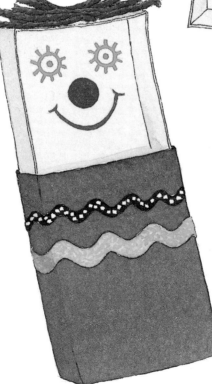

Slide the face inside the outer box. When it is time for Jack to pop out, just push on the bottom edge of the inner box.

"Won't you come out?"
"Yes, I will!"

23

Changing Face Cup Puppet

Here is what you need:

  scissors

2 plastic cups

 masking tape

 permanent markers

Here is what you do:

1 Cut out a circle, about the size of a half dollar, on the side near the bottom of one cup.

2 Wrap the bottom half of the second cup with masking tape.

1

2

24

3 Turn the wrapped cup over and place the cup with the hole over the wrapped cup. The hole will be the head. Draw a body under the head with permanent markers.

4 Draw a happy face on the masking tape showing through the hole for the head. Turn the outer cup just enough to hide the happy face and draw a sad face on the tape. Turn the cup again to draw a mad face and once more for a sleepy face. You will have room to draw just four faces. Do not turn the cup too far past each face or you will run out of space for the fourth face.

As you sing "If You're Happy and You Know It" turn the outer cup to show the correct face for each verse.

*"If you're happy and you know it
and you really want to show it..."*

25

Green and Yellow Basket Necklace

Here is what you need:

 scissors

 green labeling tape

 ruler

 green pipe cleaner

 sharp markers

 fabric scrap

 yellow plastic lid

yellow yarn

paper

 white glue

pen

Here is what you do:

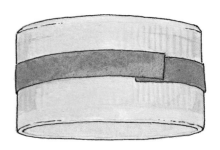

1 The yellow lid will be the basket. Add green to the basket by sticking a strip of green labeling tape around it.

2 Cut a 6-inch (15-cm) piece of pipe cleaner for the handle. Squeeze glue into the bottom of the lid basket. Set the two ends of the pipe cleaner in the glue on each side of the basket.

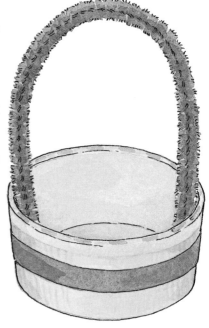

3 Cut a 3-inch (8-cm) square of fabric. Push the center of the fabric square down into the glue in the basket with the print side up.

Dear Sara,
You're great!
      -Dan
♥ ♥ ♥

4 Cut a small piece of paper for the "letter to my love." Write a little letter and decorate it with the markers. Fold the letter and put it in the basket.

5 Cut a 2-foot (61-cm) length of yellow yarn. String the yarn through the handle of the basket and tie the two ends together to form a necklace.

When you wear the green and yellow basket necklace, please be careful not to lose the letter! You might even want to glue it into the basket.

Finger Puppets of the Whole Family

Here is what you need:

 scissors

 white glue

 10 small beads and/or wiggle eyes

5 tiny pom-poms

trims

yarn scraps

5 old neckties

felt scraps

ruler

5 small pom-poms

Here is what you do:

1 Cut a 2 1/2-inch (6-cm) piece off the narrow end of each of four ties. Cut a slightly longer piece off the end of the last tie for Tall Man. Each piece will be a finger puppet of one of the characters in the song. Use the widest tie end for Thumbkin, and the narrowest one for Pinky.

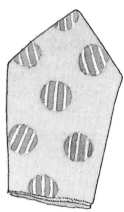

If any of the tie pieces have come open in the back, glue the seam back together.

2 Cut five 1-inch (2.5-cm) circles from different colors of felt for the faces. Glue a felt circle to each finger puppet, just below the start of the point. Glue two beads or wiggle eyes on each face. Give each man a nose by gluing a tiny pom-pom below the eyes. Give some of the puppets hair by gluing on yarn bits.

3 Glue a different piece of trim across the top of each head to form the bottom of the hat. Glue a small pom-pom to the point of each hat.

Put the appropriate puppet on each of the fingers of your left hand and hide them behind your back and sing

"Where is Thumbkin?"
"Here I am!"

29

Rocking Baby Toy

Here is what you need:

 scissors

 ruler

 white glue

 newspaper to work on

 2 small wiggle eyes

green yarn

2 cotton balls

pink pom-pom

fabric scrap

thin pink ribbon

 brown poster paint and a paintbrush

cardboard egg carton

old glove

brown construction paper

Here is what you do:

1 The glove will form the branches of a tree. Cut a 7-inch (18-cm) trunk for the tree from the brown paper. Glue the top of the trunk to the cuff of the glove.

2 Cut lots of yarn bits from the green yarn. Glue the yarn bits all over the glove and the top of the trunk for the leaves of the tree. Let the glue dry completely before putting the glove tree on your hand.

3 To make a cradle for the baby, cut two egg cups from the cardboard egg carton. Paint both cups brown, inside and out.

4 Cut a 10-inch (25-cm) length of thin pink ribbon. Tie the two ends together. Glue the knot over the bottom of one of the egg cups. Turn the second cup on its side and glue it inside one end of the bottom cup, over pink ribbon, to form the top of the cradle.

5 Glue two cotton balls in the cradle. Glue a scrap of fabric over the cotton to look like a blanket. Glue the pink pom-pom at the end of the blanket to make the head of the baby. Glue two wiggle eyes on the head.

To use the "Rock-a-bye Baby" toy, put the glove tree on one hand. Hang the cradle by the ribbon from one of the finger branches of the tree. Rock the cradle, then bend your finger down to make the cradle fall and

"...down will come baby, cradle, and all."

31

Farmer and Friends in the Dell

Here is what you need:

 large sheet of green-construction paper

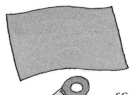 scissors

 markers

large sheet of white construction paper

 cellophane tape

Here is what you do:

1 Fold the white sheet of construction paper in half lengthwise and cut it in half on the line.

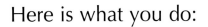

2 Draw all the characters from the song on one of the strips. You will need to draw the farmer, his wife, the child, the nurse, the dog, the cat, the rat, and the cheese. You need to start on the right side of the strip and draw them in order, going from right to left.

3 A dell is a small valley, usually with trees in it. On the green paper, draw an outdoor scene of what you think the farmer's dell might look like.

4 Cut a 6 1/2-inch (16.5-cm)-long slit 1 inch (2.5 cm) from each side of the green paper.

5 Tape the second strip of white paper to the right side of the paper strip with the characters on it. Thread the strip through the back of the green paper, across the front, and back through the second slit to form a continuous strip. Tape the two ends of the strip together on both sides.

Arrange the strip so that all the characters are at the back of the paper. As you sing each verse of the song, move that character through the slit to the front of the paper. For the last verse slide all the characters through the second slit to the back of the paper—except for the cheese, of course!

"The cheese stands alone."

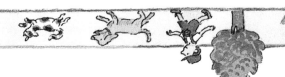

Tippy Teapot

Here is what you need:

 scissors

old knit glove

 masking tape

 2 large wiggle eyes

 6-inch (15-cm) paper bowl

12-inch (30-cm) pipe cleaner

 white glue

 1-inch (2.5-cm) pom-pom

 trims

 red marker

 flower stickers

Here is what you do:

1 Cut the middle finger off the old glove. Use masking tape to attach the end of the finger to the rim of the bowl to form the spout of the teapot.

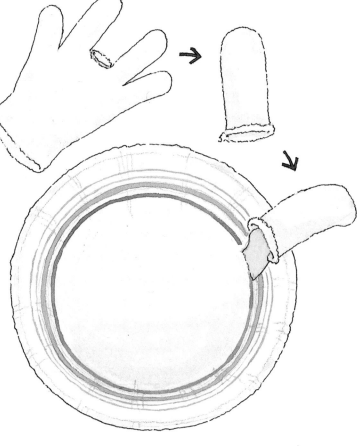

2 Bend the pipe cleaner in half. Twist it together to hold the fold. Tape the two ends of the folded pipe cleaner to the rim of the opposite side of the bowl to make the handle of the teapot.

3 Glue the two wiggle eyes to the upper portion of the bottom of the bowl. Use the red marker to give the teapot a big smile.

4 Glue the pom-pom to the top edge of the teapot to look like the handle of the lid of the pot.

5 Decorate the teapot using trims and pretty flower stickers.

Hold the teapot by the handle with one hand and put the pointer finger of your other hand into the spout.

"...tip me over, pour me out."

35

Your Own Pretty Horse

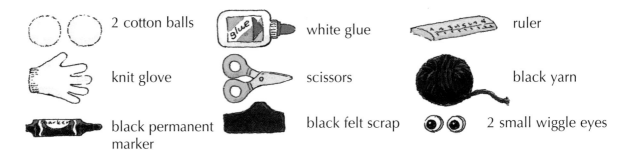

Here is what you need:

2 cotton balls

white glue

ruler

knit glove

scissors

black yarn

black permanent marker

black felt scrap

2 small wiggle eyes

Here is what you do:

1 Stuff the two cotton balls into the end of the middle finger of the glove to form a head for the horse, with the unstuffed portion of the finger forming the neck. The remaining thumb and three fingers will become the legs.

2 Use the marker to draw nostrils on the end of the head. Glue on the two wiggle eyes, about 1 inch (2.5 cm) back from the nostrils.

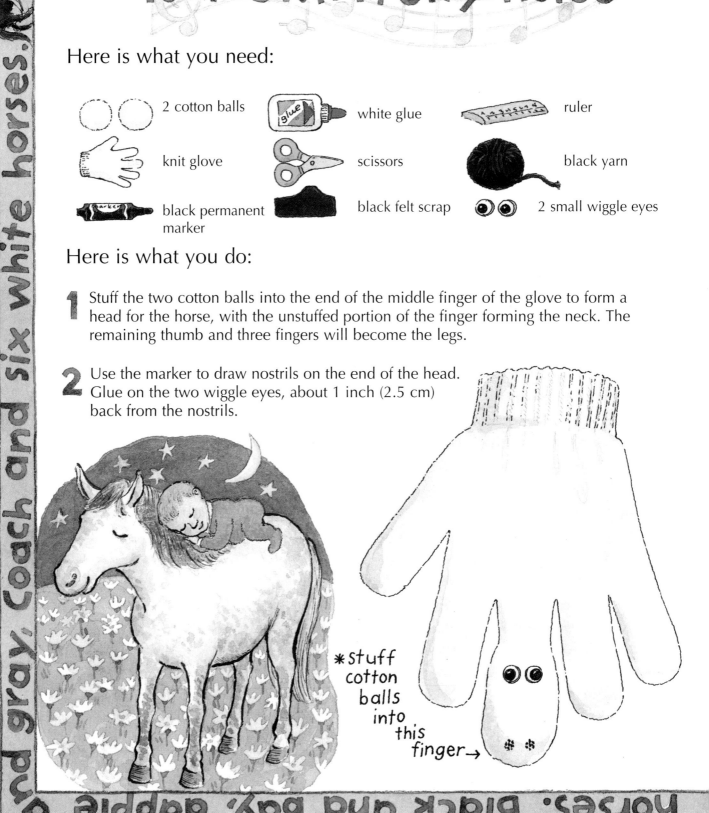

*stuff cotton balls into this finger→

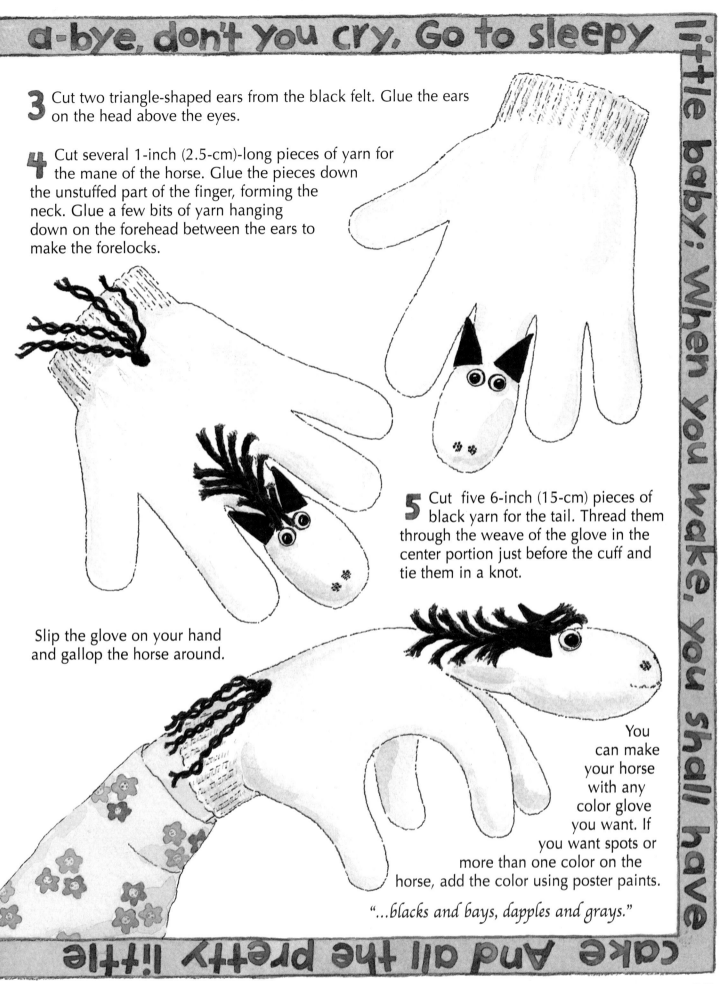

3 Cut two triangle-shaped ears from the black felt. Glue the ears on the head above the eyes.

4 Cut several 1-inch (2.5-cm)-long pieces of yarn for the mane of the horse. Glue the pieces down the unstuffed part of the finger, forming the neck. Glue a few bits of yarn hanging down on the forehead between the ears to make the forelocks.

5 Cut five 6-inch (15-cm) pieces of black yarn for the tail. Thread them through the weave of the glove in the center portion just before the cuff and tie them in a knot.

Slip the glove on your hand and gallop the horse around.

You can make your horse with any color glove you want. If you want spots or more than one color on the horse, add the color using poster paints.

"...blacks and bays, dapples and grays."

37

Bug Eating Frog on a Log

Here is what you need:

 scissors

 white glue

small card-board tube

 black and brown markers

 masking tape

2 small white pom-poms

 green flip-open plastic top from salad-dressing bottle

6-inch (15-cm) red pipe cleaner

seed bead

Here is what you do:

1 Cut down the side of the cardboard tube. Cut a 1-inch (2.5-cm) strip out of the side of the tube and discard it. The remaining tube will be the log for the frog. Use the brown marker to color it, or just add some lines to look like bark.

2 The green lid will become the frog. Put a small piece of masking tape on top of the lid to create a better gluing surface. Glue the two pom-poms on the top of the lid for the eyes. Use the black marker to give each eye a pupil.

3 The red pipe cleaner will be the tongue of the frog. Thread the seed bead onto one end of the pipe cleaner for the "bug" and fold the end down to hold it in place.

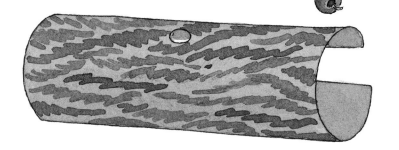

4 Hold the tube so that the opening is in the back. Poke a small hole in the center of the top of the tube.

5 Open the top of the lid to look like a frog with an open mouth. Use the masking tape on the back of the frog to tape it on the log, with the hole inside the lid directly over the hole in the log.

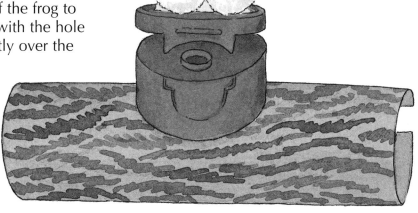

6 Thread the end of the pipe cleaner tongue without the bead down through the hole in the lid and the cardboard tube so that the end comes out behind the tube.

You should now be able to move the tongue of the frog in and out of the open mouth.

"...eating some most delicious bugs, yum yum!"

People on the Bus
Going up and down

Here is what you need:

scissors

ruler

1 lb. spaghetti box

ballpoint pen

pipe cleaner

 4 pasta wheels

masking tape

stickers

markers

clamp clothespin

 white glue

labeling tape

paper

aluminum foil

Here is what you do:

1 Cut off the end of the spaghetti box so that the remaining part is 7 inches (18 cm) long and is the end with a window in it. This will be the bus.

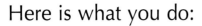

2 Cover the bus with aluminum foil. Use masking tape to hold down the ends of the foil. Rub your finger over the foil until you find the window of the box. Rub around the window to make an outline of it in the foil. Gently go around the outline of the window with the point of the ballpoint pen to cut out the foil to expose the see-through window of the box.

3 Cut two 3-inch (8-cm) pieces of pipe cleaner for the wheel axles. Put a pasta wheel on each end and fold down the end of the pipe cleaner to hold each wheel in place.

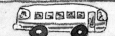 
Use the masking tape to tape the axles across the bottom of the bus, one toward the front and the other toward the back.

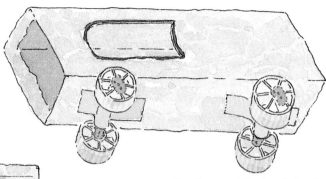

4 Decorate the bus with the labeling tape and stickers. If you want to draw something on the bus you will need to use permanent markers. Otherwise, put some masking tape over the foil and draw on the tape.

5 Cut a piece of paper that is a little wider than the window and twice as long. Fold the paper in half lengthwise. Along the top fold of the paper, use the markers to draw people looking out the bus window.

6 Glue the bottom fold of the paper to one side of the clamp clothespin. Glue the clothespin inside the open end of the bus so that the people are looking out the window.

Pinch the end of the clothespin to move the people up and down.

"The people on the bus go up and down..."

Washed-Out Spider

Here is what you need:

 scissors

short and long cardboard tubes

black pipe cleaners

black marker

 cellophane tape

 1/2 (1.25 cm) inch wooden bead

 masking tape

 silver tinsel

black yarn

 aluminum foil

Here is what you do:

1 Cut a slit halfway down the side of the short tube. Overlap the two sides of the cut tube and use the cellophane tape to hold the sides together. Slide the uncut end of the short tube up into one end of the long tube to look like the bent end of a waterspout. Tape it in place. If the short tube does not fit into the longer tube, just cut partway down the opposite side from the side you already cut, and overlap the cut ends to make it small enough around to fit inside.

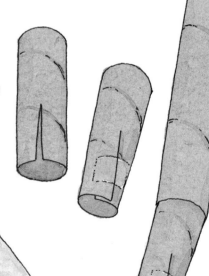

2 Cover the entire tube with aluminum foil to make the waterspout. Use cellophane tape to hold loose ends in place.

3 Color the bead with the black marker to make the body of a spider. Put a small piece of masking tape on the side of the bead and draw two eyes.

4 Cut a 3-foot (91-cm) length of yarn. Tie the bead to one end of the yarn. Slide four 2-inch (5-cm) pipe cleaner pieces through the holes in the bead to make the eight legs for the spider.

5 Tie the center of some silver tinsel to the yarn about 7 inches (18 cm) up from the spider so that it hangs down on each side of the tie. Tie another bunch about 5 inches (13 cm) up from the first bunch. Trim the tinsel on each side to about 3 to 4 inches (8 to 10 cm) long. This will be the rain that comes down on the spider.

Drop the spider end of the yarn down through the top of the spout so that it comes out the bottom bent end of the spout. Hold the spout in one hand and the end of the yarn in the other hand. Start with just the spider hanging down out of the spout. Pull the yarn to bring the spider up into the spout. Lower the yarn to bring the spider and the rain down out of the tube. Pull the rain back up inside when the sun dries it, then, finally, pull the spider back up into the spout again.

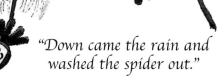

"Down came the rain and washed the spider out."

43

Find Bo Peep's Sheep Wheel

Here is what you need:

 newspaper to work on

scissors

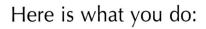 ruler

paper fastener

 2 paper plates, 9-inch (23-cm)

 markers

3 cotton balls

black pipe cleaner

 blue and green poster paint and a paintbrush

 white paper

 white glue

Here is what you do:

1 Paint the eating side of one of the paper plates blue for sky.

2 Cut a little less than half of the inner circle out of the second paper plate to create a window. Paint the eating side of the cut plate blue around the curved edge of the window and green for the grass below it. Let the plates dry.

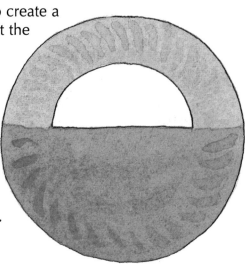

3 On the white paper draw a picture of little Bo Peep that is about 4 inches (10 cm) tall. Cut the picture out. Glue Bo Peep standing on one side of the green grass part of the cut plate.

4 Attach the cut plate over the blue plate by putting the paper fastener through the center of both plates.

5 Make sheep by gluing three cotton balls on the portion of the back plate showing through the window. Cut bits of black pipe cleaner for the head and legs of the sheep and glue them in place. Let the glue dry.

When the back plate is turned, the sheep can be hidden behind the first plate. They can be made to reappear by continuing to turn the back plate until they show in the window of the top plate again.

"Little Bo Peep has lost her sheep…"

And can't tell where to find

45

BINGO Marker Can

Here is what you need:

scissors

brown paper bag

black marker

sticky-back magnets

5 pry-off type bottle caps

black and white plus five other colors of construction paper scraps

white glue

small coffee can

cellophane tape

hole punch

Here is what you do:

1 Cut a piece from the brown bag big enough to cover the outside of the can. If the can has a paper label you can remove it and use it for a pattern. Otherwise, cut a piece that is slightly larger than the can, wrap it around the can, and trim it to fit. Use tape to hold the paper in place.

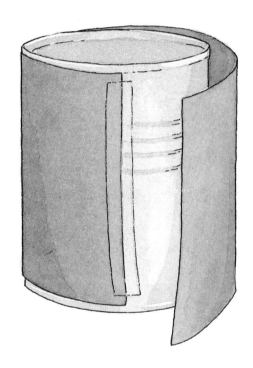

2 Cut two long, floppy dog ears from the brown paper to go on each side of the top of the can.

3 Fold the top end of each ear back and tape it inside the can to hold each ear in place.

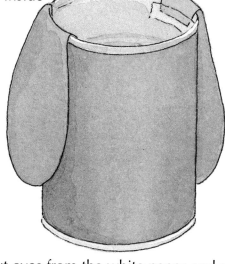

4 Cut eyes from the white paper and pupils for the eyes from the black paper. Glue the pupils to the eyes, then glue the eyes on the upper portion of the can between the ears.

5 Cut a nose from the black paper and glue it on below the eyes. Use the marker to draw a mouth below the nose. Use the hole punch to make several "freckles" for each side of the face of the dog.

6 Cut a 1-inch (2.5-cm) circle from each of the five colors of construction paper.

7 Write one letter from the word B-I-N-G-O on each circle. Glue a circle inside each bottle cap. Cut a piece of sticky-back magnet for the back of each of the five caps and stick them in place.

Stick the caps on the front of the dog can to spell BINGO. As you sing the song you can remove a letter for each verse and drop it in the can. This can is also perfect for holding markers and other small items.

"...and BINGO was his name-o."

About the Author and Artist

Thirty years as a teacher and director of nursery school programs in Oneida, New York, have given Kathy Ross extensive experience in guiding children through craft projects. A collector of teddy bears and paper dolls, her craft projects have frequently appeared in *Highlights* magazine. She is the author of The Millbrook Press's Holiday Crafts for Kids series and the Crafts for Kids Who Are Wild About series. She is also the author of *Gifts to Make for Your Favorite Grown-ups, The Best Holiday Craft Book Ever, Crafts for Kids Who Are Wild About the Wild, The Best Birthday Parties Ever: A Kid's Do-It-Yourself Guide, Christmas Ornaments Kids Can Make, Christmas Decorations Kids Can Make, More Christmas Ornaments Kids Can Make, Make Yourself a Monster,* and *Crafts from Your Favorite Bible Stories.*

Vicky Enright is an illustrator living in Andover, Massachusetts, with a small son, two huge labrador retriever dogs, and her husband. To date, she has utilized her talents as a calligrapher, a wallpaper designer, and a greeting card artist. Her first book was *Crafts From Your Favorite Fairy Tales* by Kathy Ross. She is the illustrator of *Crafts to Make in the Spring, Crafts to Make in the Summer, Crafts to Make in the Fall, Crafts to Make in the Winter,* and *Crafts for All Seasons.*